Praise from Industry Leaders

"ERGs are the lifeblood of every organization's culture. The expert insights in Alyssa's book will assist every company seeking to invest, support and connect their employees in deeply meaningful ways."

Meredith Morales (she, her)
Global ERG Recognition Programs Lead
Diversity, Inclusion, Belonging (DIBs)
LinkedIn

"This is timely work as it gives a thorough roadmap on what, when, why and how to build ERGs that work strategically within your organization. As diversity officers, we struggle with meaningful metrics; you will find them here. It is a great resource that will be bookmarked for years by those who want to get it right."

Darlene Slaughter (she, her)
VP, Chief Diversity, Inclusion & Engagement Officer
March of Dimes

"When done right, ERGs promote employee engagement, and this book helps you get them on track and ready to thrive!"

Rogelio Guzman (he, him)
DEI Program Director, Office of Diversity, Equity & Inclusion
Mass General Brigham

"ERG Intelligence is coming out at a critical time for leaders. ERGs are no longer nice to have but a MUST-have for any business taking DEI work seriously. Whether your organization is just starting on its ERG journey or has multiple ERGs, you will find the necessary actions for ERG success are laid out nicely in a comprehensive and easy-to-understand narrative. ERG Intelligence was written to help ensure that your ERGs are making a business impact while simultaneously helping your organization be a great place to work."

Chantal Roche (she, her)
Director, Inclusion & Diversity
Staples

"Employee Resource Groups are an essential way to engage staff and bring our whole selves to work—especially as we strive for reproductive rights as a fundamental human right."

JP Pierre (she, her)
Chief Diversity, Equity, & Inclusion Officer (CDEIO)
Center for Reproductive Rights

"For every leadership level, ERG Intelligence provides an easy-to-digest explanation of why and how employee groups are critical to enabling sustainable diversity, equity, and inclusion."

Marinda Monfilston (she, her)
Office of Diversity & Inclusion
Yale University

"This is an excellent book to understand how to leverage ERGs, so they serve stakeholders and drive business results."

Eduardo Arabu (he, him)
Chief Executive Officer
National Hispanic Corporate Council & Latino DEI Collective

"Whether you think you know, or you're simply curious about the value of employee groups, this book will provide a quick education about the benefit to the employees and precisely why these groups are critical to every type of organization."

Maria A. Killian MBA, PMP© (she, her)
2017 – 2021 President, Technical Women's Organization
Federal Aviation Administration (FAA)

ERG Intelligence

What Every Leader Needs To Know About Employee Groups

Alyssa Dver

Mind Full Press
a subsidiary of Z. Holden Bros. Publishing Group

Copyright © 2022, 2023 by Alyssa Dver

Published in the United States by Mind Full Press, a subsidiary of Z. Holden Bros. Publishing Group.

ISBN: 978-0-9833927-9-8 (Paperback, 2nd edition)
ISBN: 979-8-9888931-0-3 (Kindle eBook, 2nd edition)

All rights reserved. Except as permitted under the United States Copyright Act, no part of this publication may be reproduced or distributed in any form or by any means or stored in a database or retrieval system without the prior written permission of the copyright holders.

Company and product names mentioned herein are the trademarks or registered trademarks of their respective owners.

ERG Intelligence books are available at special quantity discounts for corporations, not-for-profit organizations and academic use.

www.ERGLeadershipAlliance.com

info@ERGLeadershipAlliance.com

10 9 8 7 6 5 4 3 2 1

*The best way to get confidence
is to give it to others.*

Contents

Introduction   11
   What You Will Learn in This Book   13
   Why Listen to Me?   14

Section 1: What Are Employee Groups?   17
   What Defines an Employee Group?   19
   How Do Employee Groups Differ from Labor Unions?   21
   What Are the Various Names of Employee Groups?   22
   What Are the Typical Types or Categories of Employee Groups?   24
   What Types of Organizations Have Employee Groups?   26
   Who Participates in an Employee Group?   27
   Who Is Affected by Employee Groups?   32
   What Is the Typical Structure of an Employee Group Leadership Team?   33
   Do Leaders Get Paid?   36
   How Do You Measure Employee Group Success?   39

Section 2: Why Employee Groups Matter   41
   What Is the Purpose of Employee Groups?   43
   How Are Employee Groups Visible?   48
   Why Are Employee Groups So Popular Now?   51

Section 3: Where Employee Groups Are Now and Where They're Going Next   53
   What Is the General State of Employee Groups Today?   55
   What Are the Minimum Requirements to Start Employee Groups?   56
   What Controversial Issues Should be Considered?   60
   How Do You Know Whether Your Organization Is Ready to Start Employee Groups?   61

How Do You Know if Employee Groups Will Make a Positive Difference?   62
Trends & Transformations in Employee Groups   64
What's Coming Next?   78
What Can You Do Right Now?   79

Appendix A: Template for Creating an Employee Group Policy & Procedures Guide   81

Message From the CEO/CHRO/DEI Lead   83
Our Organization's Overall ERGs' Mission and Purpose   83
Our Employee Group Application & Acceptance Process   84
Your Employee Group Mission and Goals   84
Your Employee Group Structure   85
Your Employee Group Governance Requirements   85
Launching Your Employee Group   87
The Employee Group Budget and Funding Process   87
Communicating with Your Members   88
Communicating with Other Employee Group Supporters   88
How to Recruit Employee Group Members   89
How to Recruit ERG Allies   89
How to Plan & Run Employee Group Leadership Meetings   90
How to Plan & Run Employee Group Programming   90
Leadership Tips   91

Appendix B: Sample Agenda for an Employee Group Leadership Summit   93
Acknowledgments   97
About ERG Leadership Alliance (ELA)   99

Introduction

Just by reading this book, you can make a significant difference for everyone in your organization, as well as an impact on the lives of over 41 million people already involved with employee groups around the world.[1,2] Whether you participate as an employee group member, leader, oversight manager, executive sponsor or ally, you will help make every workplace more diverse, equitable and inclusive.

Employee groups enable psychological safety. When employees know they belong and feel connected to the organization, they can more comfortably bring their whole selves to work and contribute with their optimal creativity and commitment.

Employee groups are an essential employee benefit to attract and retain diverse talent. Each type of group functions as a leadership development sandbox and helps to identify high-potential leaders.

And more than just for the members, employee groups build overall positive organizational cultures that welcome customers and other critical stakeholders.

As the book will describe, well-run employee groups aim to harmonize employer and employee needs. As such, the groups must navigate the paradoxical requirements for each group's unique identity to be appreciated while being integrated and held accountable within a greater organizational ecosystem.

---

[1] According to NAICS, 164,211 businesses have more than 1,000 employees. They are, therefore, likely to have ERGs X 5 ERGs on average = 821,055 ERGs X 50 people per ERG on average = 41,052,750 million people directly involved in the US alone.

[2] "US Business Firmographics – Company Size." NAICS Association, https://www.naics.com/business-lists/counts-by-company-size/.

Intellectually fascinating, these groups have been operating in relative stealth for more than 60 years but are changing at a staggering pace. We are only understanding now what well-run employee groups do and what they contribute. It is clear through emerging academic research and annual corporate surveys that when employee groups are done well - and not simply added as "color-washed" diversity optics - they powerfully and positively impact the overall health of the business and everyone in it.

This book is designed for anyone who wants quick explanations of fundamental employee group concepts and considerations. It will help you understand what today's employee groups are, what they do and the critical strategic issues to consider so you and your entire organization can proceed effectively.

Appendix A provides a complete template to create or compare your organization's ERG Policy & Procedures Guide to assist you in setting overall governance and guidance for strong and sustainable employee groups. Appendix B is a Sample Agenda for an Employee Group Leadership Summit, a trend quickly becoming standard ERG oversight practice.

This book isn't intended to critique how well your current groups are functioning, nor will it provide you with individual group operational and planning details. You will, however, be prepared for the often paradoxical and passion-driven questions that do not have a single right answer—or even best practice.

My goal is to give you the confidence to participate within your organization's employee group ecosystem in whatever way is best for you right now.

Therefore, please use and freely share this book so that together we can enable better work experiences and bottom-line results for all.

What You Will Learn in This Book

- What are employee groups and their business purpose
- The various names, types and structures of employee groups
- What types of organizations have or should have employee groups
- Who is involved, why do they choose to participate, and how are they, and everyone else, affected by employee groups
- Critical and controversial considerations for setting up employee groups
- Cross-industry employee group trends, common policies and operating practices
- Next steps to advance your organization's employee groups

Why Listen to Me?

Since founding the ERG Leadership Alliance (ELA) in 2019, I've actively listened to and worked with thousands of employee groups around the world. My team and I interview several hundred employee group champions every month and have conducted our own, as well as contributed to and collected other real-world research.

However, my experience with employee groups extends to more than a decade through the many presentations I have done in my "day job" as CEO of the American Confidence Institute (ACI). As I frequently delivered keynotes and workshops to employee groups, I found surprising and unexplainable inconsistencies. There was no correlation given the organizations' industries, sizes or ages, nor even between employee groups within a single organization.

Employee group success was a direct result of a committed volunteer leadership team that was serendipitously in place at that moment. And unfortunately, the groups often fell apart over time when those leaders moved on, whether because they'd reached a term limit or left the organization altogether. Few groups tracked metrics to show success or had the governance documentation necessary to avoid internal conflicts and address inefficiencies.

There was sporadic executive support (often, these leaders were "voluntold" to participate), and little awareness of the group was shared with others in the organization. When I asked senior talent management leaders why they thought this might be, they told me employee groups were only good for "food, flags and fun." No wonder the groups were commonly underfunded and regarded as social clubs!

Yet, I always found the groups led by passionate, persistent individuals. And when I asked about why and how they were run, I received varied answers but common frustrations. It was clear that these groups needed fundamental business help, including concrete ways to operate, plan, measure and communicate progress to the entire organization. It was shocking that for over 60 years, no one paid attention to the untapped, high-potential talent and powerful cultural levers enabled by employee groups.[3]

Thankfully, I didn't listen to the pessimists, and ELA has over 25,000 community members at the time of this writing. ERG champions around the world have taken advantage of the resources, training and connections we offer. They actively participate in our events, including the annual ERG International Symposia and frequent ERG Learning Labs. We've trained thousands of group leaders, executive sponsors and allies from many of the best-known U.S. and non-U.S. brands. And perhaps surprisingly, many ELA members are non-profit organizations, including academic institutions and government agencies.

Further evidence that the market is reaching its full potential is the number of ERG leaders and expert trainers seeking to get certified as proof of their ability and credentials for future career paths. The ELA Job Board is now filled with DEI and ERG-specific opportunities, while our ERG Appreciation Shout Outs help showcase the inspiring work.

As "The ERG of ERGs," ELA created the *Oversight Managers Group (OMG)*™ membership that provides a safe space for full-time, program-level professionals to collaborate and commiserate in monthly masterminds, an online private community and an annual summit of their own. With this group, industry policy and processes are being co-created, paving the way for employee groups to be woven into every organization's culture and business decisions.

---

[3] Xerox is credited with starting the first employee groups in the 1960s.

ELA celebrates and supports organizations recognizing the business and societal opportunities that inclusivity enables. These DEI-committed organizations know that employee groups are at the center of their employee experience and talent management strategies. *They realize that employee groups are no longer nice-to-have extras but are necessary to attract, retain and engage critical talent. Employee groups directly impact the bottom line since they improve the entire culture, productivity, and well-being of everyone in the organization.*

If you don't have employee groups already, stop reading this book. Focus first on examining your recruitment, engagement and other culture benchmarks. If you already appreciate that your employees expect to work for more than just a paycheck, please continue reading this book to learn what you need to know – and do – right now.

If you and your organization haven't already, I invite you to join our community:

www.ERGLeadershipAlliance.com

Section 1: What Are Employee Groups?

What Defines an Employee Group?

Employee groups are essentially employee-led but organization-assisted associations within a business, academic institution, government or non-profit entity. Different from a club, employee groups receive funding from the organization. As a result, employee groups are required to have some governance and accountability.

Funding might come in the form of an annual budget tied to a submitted programming plan or as the result of ad hoc requests to arrange specific events or professional training. Funding can vary from group to group and can be tied to an expected return on investment (ROI), number of members or distributed more arbitrarily.

Employee groups typically have a defined leadership structure and welcome anyone who wants to be a member, even if the individual's identity is outside the group's target demographics. Members can be defined loosely as employees who at least opt into the group's mailing list or communication platform, or more telling, individuals who attend at least some of the group's events. An employee group usually has at least one executive sponsor and, ideally, many allies.

Clear governance with at least a documented charter and set of operating procedures is critical to ensure equity and reduce organizational liabilities. Procedures should include formal requirements for forming new groups, agreed-upon metrics that will be collected and how they will be reported, and sanctioned communication channels and processes used to promote the groups to existing employees, candidates and other stakeholders. Leaders and executive sponsors should clearly understand their responsibilities and objectives. Allies and others in the organization should be invited and informed about how they can support the groups, too. Perhaps the most critical yet often overlooked aspect of ERG leadership is clarity on the personal 'why' the person is choosing to lead and some idea of who can carry their legacy forward once the leader is done with their leadership role.[4]

---

[4] ELA offers six (6) ERG Blueprints™ that are two- or three-page fillable PDFs to help learn and plan each of the operating areas.

How Do Employee Groups Differ from Labor Unions?

Both employee groups and labor unions are intended to give employees a powerful voice to advocate for things they need or want from the organization. Both employee groups and labor unions have leadership structures and governance. Both provide a sense of belonging and some psychological safety. However, there are four main differences between these types of associations.

1. Employee groups are funded by the organization they serve. As such, they must typically present a business case for existing and demonstrate subsequent return on investment (ROI) and alignment with the organization's diversity goals.
2. Joining an employee group is optional, and employees can join multiple groups. Employees voluntarily participate in any activities an employee group offers, whether the employee is an official member, prospective member or ally.
3. Employee groups are not established to represent employees in negotiations with management but to support business and diversity objectives. In fact, well-run employee groups become integral to many business decisions. The groups provide professional development and career mobility for employees and assist the organization in recruiting and onboarding new employees.
4. While labor unions remain important in representing employee rights, employee groups aim to educate and foster cultural change within the organization. Employee groups can be perceived to be softer, patriarchal or even corporate-controlled. Still, well-run employee group programs work hard to balance employees' and employers' needs.

What Are the Various Names of Employee Groups?

Employee groups are known by many names:
- *Employee Resource Groups (ERGs)* is the most often used term.
- *Business Resource Groups (BRGs)* reinforce group alignment with business objectives.
- *Associate Resource Groups (ARGs), Colleague Resource Groups (CRGs)* or *Member Resource Groups (MRGs)* reflect how the organization refers to its employees.
- *Employee Networks* or *Employee Associations*
- *Inclusion Resource Groups (IRGs)* or *Networking Resource Groups (NRGs)*
- *Affinity Groups*, which typically refer to more informal groups
- Many others!

For this book, we will continue to refer to all types as *employee groups or ERGs*.

While naming conventions can be interchangeable, the choice often reflects the organization's stance on how the employee groups should prioritize their activities and how the rest of the organization should leverage them. Using the term "business resource groups," for example, can imply that the group's activities are expected to contribute directly to business objectives quantitatively. Using "employee networks" or "affinity groups" suggests a focus on community-building. It's not unusual for organizations to change from one moniker to another.

Some organizations have multiple types or categories of groups defined by their unique purposes and policies. For example, an organization might have ERGs mapped to diversity initiatives and affinity groups to facilitate a community around shared hobbies or other interests. The overarching name for the employee groups does not indicate whether they receive funding or the requirements for reporting their progress and plans. The naming, types and requirements of an organization's employee groups largely depend on the organization's leadership at a point in time.

What Are the Typical Types or Categories of Employee Groups?

Here are the most common, but by no means all, types of employee groups:
- Women
- Black, Indigenous or People of Color (BIPOC)
- Hispanic or LatinX
- Lesbian, gay, bisexual, transgender, queer et al. (LGBTQ+)
- Veterans
- Disabled
- Asian, Pacific Islanders
- Young professionals
- Cross or multigenerational
- Neurodiverse
- Caregivers
- Community focused
- Charitable causes
- Religious
- Political
- Hobbyists (e.g., knitting, bridge or birdwatching)
- Skill-based (e.g., Toastmasters, which is an organized, professional development program for people who want to improve their public speaking and leadership skills)

There are many generally accepted, politically correct ways to categorize the target demographics of employee groups. Some people will refer to the targeted demographics as "underserved," "underrepresented," "historically excluded," or "protected classes." These terms may or may not be appropriate in various instances.

There are also questions about who qualifies as a "target population" for employee groups. The U.S. government's websites vary regarding who is eligible for diverse supplier certification, government spending set-asides and other business incentives. When challenged that groups such as Toastmasters should not be treated in the same way as the Black or Hispanic groups, some leaders argue that if a group exists to build professional connections, improve professional skills and support the well-being of a set of likeminded employees, why is that gathering any less aligned with the purpose of other employee groups? As another example, young professionals need professional development, connection and mentoring just as any of the groups; yet as a group type, they would never be called "underserved" or "minority."

The Diversity, Equity and Inclusion (DEI) Office will typically define each organization's sanctioned groups. Ideally, the organization will clearly state what types of employee groups can apply for formation, funding and formal recognition. The rules to start and run an employee group should be documented in an Employee Group Policy & Procedures Guide or similarly titled governance document that states the requirements for forming and running an official, recognized and funded employee group.

Employee group policy documents should be revisited and edited every few months to reflect the culture and learnings of your organization as well as the rapid development happening in the employee group 'industry.'

See page 81, Appendix A for an Employee Group Policy & Procedures Guide Template that compiles over fifty (50) employee groups' policy documents. Use the template to create a new policy document or as a checklist for an ERG policy document you already have.

What Types of Organizations Have Employee Groups?

Using ERG Leadership Alliance's (ELA's) community as a statistically significant data set, it's clear that organizations of every size, industry and location have employee groups. All types of organizations, including corporations, non-profits, municipalities, federal agencies and academic institutions, have employee groups. Organizations with employee groups range from those with as few as thirty total employees to those with hundreds of thousands of employees worldwide.

Today, most organizations with active employee groups are based in the United States and may have operations in multiple domestic and international locations. However, many organizations headquartered outside the U.S. have or are launching employee groups. Those groups vary in purpose and form, often as a function of culture and reflecting the local social and political environment.

There is no single factor, such as an organization's revenue, number of employees, number of locations or any other metric that determines its number, strength, longevity or funding of employee groups. An organization's culture and talent strategy will determine if and how employee groups develop.

Who Participates in an Employee Group?

The Role of Members

A member can be defined in a variety of ways, such as someone who Is on a group mailing list or based on their program participation. Members are any employees who may or may not represent the group type itself. Since employee groups are inclusive by definition, membership and program participation should be open to anyone interested. For example, men can opt to join a women's group, though they can alternatively affiliate as allies. However, it is critical to define whom the group is intended to serve, why the group is necessary for this population and the expected impact the group will have on those specific people. While allies should be welcome to support and participate in most (but not all) activities, the group exists for its members, who should consistently experience a safe space that recognizes their personal and professional needs.

The Role of Leaders

A group will typically have multiple leaders (*See page 33, What Is the Typical Structure of an Employee Group Leadership Team?*) Leaders are employees who typically volunteer to serve an employee group in addition to their regular, paid or hired jobs. (*See page 36, Do Leaders Get Paid?*) A leader (or, more commonly, a co-leader) may or may have different demographics than the group's membership. For example, though not typical, someone who is not gay or transgender—but committed as an ally—could be a co-leader of an LGBTQ+ group.

Leadership scope should be geographically defined such that a leader can be responsible for more than a single group within a single country (e.g., U.S., France) or region (e.g., Europe, Asia-Pacific) or have global leadership oversight for a type of group (e.g., women, Indigenous People).

There should be a documented process for application, selection or election of all group leadership roles. Leadership structure can include one or two leaders (commonly called the "chairs") plus others supporting the group *(See page 33, What Is the Typical Structure of an Employee Group Leadership Team?)*. Leaders should have term limits with clearly defined responsibilities. Well-run groups have annual goals, membership targets, leadership succession and development plans.

The Role of Program or Oversight Managers

Organizations with more than five employee groups usually have a salaried employee group oversight manager (a "program manager" or one of dozens of other titles) responsible for coordinating across all groups. The responsibility can be the entire or only part of this individual's job. Oversight managers are responsible for setting overall employee group policies and processes, coordinating programming, and ensuring alignment with DEI and business initiatives. Oversight management can be particularly challenging given that the leaders all have direct-report managers in their "hired" jobs. Therefore, oversight managers must know how to coach and influence the leaders and all other group contributors.

The oversight manager position usually reports to the diversity function, which typically is part of human resources. Many progressive organizations, however, have a Diversity Office reporting directly to the CEO to ensure the function has visibility and influence across the entire organization.

Larger organizations often form a program office consisting of multiple oversight managers, each responsible for a specific function (e.g., leader recognition or selection) within a geography (e.g., Europe or Asia) or some other subset of the groups. In some organizations, the oversight managers reside in various geographic locations to better represent and support local groups.

The Role of Executive Sponsors

Each employee group must have at least one executive sponsor, a senior manager, often at the C-suite level. Executive sponsors volunteer or are assigned to serve as advisors and advocates. An executive sponsor's ability to contribute or fundraise can be a factor in their election or decision to take on the role. In some cases, executive sponsors will support more than one group and may have different demographics than the members. For example, a male could be an executive sponsor for a women's employee group.

The executive sponsor should personally align with the group's membership whenever possible. They should have a clear reason why that group is meaningful to them. The sponsor may have a family member or friend that aligns with the group's mission. Maybe the sponsor wants to remove obstacles they struggled to overcome in their career journey. A clear purpose for sponsoring and freely communicating with a group is critical to executive sponsor success.

If no executives match, that is an obvious sign that these employees are underrepresented in the organization's management structure. It is also a potential opportunity for those executives to gain awareness of that group's perspectives.

Executive sponsors should not manage the groups! They should provide coaching and thought partnership to help prioritize programming and overall group activity. Executive sponsors need to be internal advocates, which means they should represent and communicate about the group's success, needs and activities wherever appropriate, including executive meetings. Executive sponsors should not just speak for, but they should also arrange for the group leaders to be invited to participate in business decisions and have opportunities to directly inform other executives about the group's status and plans.

While the Diversity Office or HR function typically awards ERG funding, executive sponsors often help their group(s) obtain funding and other critical support. In addition to meeting regularly and otherwise interacting with the group's leadership team, executive sponsors should attend at least some group events to become familiar with and show support for members.

Executive sponsors should have term limits and are never compensated for their work. The role should be an opportunity to give back to and make work better for other people. The role can be emotionally taxing and even present some career challenges since it requires the executive to balance their own values with the needs of both the organization and the group.

Employee group leaders and executive sponsors should have clear communication protocols and expectations of one another's roles and responsibilities. Many organizations now provide training for executive sponsors. Some have even created a forum or group where executive sponsors can convene to offer support and share experiences. (This is an ERG for executive sponsors!)

The Role of Allies

Some individuals want to be affiliated with an employee group but are unable or unwilling to make a leadership or membership commitment at a particular time. This desire for arm's-length affiliation might result from any number of factors: a lack of available time, concerns about the impact on job performance, or discomfort with publicly declaring one's identity (e.g., someone not ready to come out as a member of the LGBTQ+ community.)

Allies can still advocate for the groups they support and participate in some of the group's activities. For example, heterosexual colleagues can show their allyship by attending a gay pride parade. While yet to be common, a handful of organizations have defined official ally programs that offer specific ways allies can be involved and recognized for their support.

Who Is Affected by Employee Groups?

Employee group information often appears in job postings and employer portals. The groups are typically highlighted in the career section of websites and covered in annual Corporate Social Responsibility (CSR) and Environmental, Social and Governance (ESG) reports. In a few impressive organizations, board members participate in select employee group events to gain awareness and offer their influential support.

While there are yet studies to detail how employee group performance quantitatively correlates to an organization's share price or valuation, I would argue that anyone involved with the organization—even indirectly—benefits from the positive cultural impacts of employee groups.

Employee groups directly impact every employee and indirectly affect customers, suppliers and other external stakeholders. Vendors/suppliers must often show proof of their diversity ownership and management representation. Customers interact with happier and more relatable organization representatives. Plus, employee groups can be effective ambassadors within the communities and for the organization's charitable partners.

With this far-reaching impact, it is critical to have a clearly communicated management structure and governance model, starting with well-defined leadership titles, responsibilities and common terms.

What Is the Typical Structure of an Employee Group Leadership Team?

A group leadership team structure will reflect the needs and interests of the group at any given time. The role titles and the scope of responsibilities may also change to best leverage the leaders' skills, available time and the group's current needs. Therefore, the team structure will likely change over time and may not even be consistent across an organization's own groups.

ELA has defined six (6) key areas of leadership team responsibility: [5]
- Defining group purpose, leadership process & roles
- Arranging programming that supports member, DEI & business objectives
- Informing & engaging all ERG stakeholders
- Collecting & reporting critical group metrics
- Onboarding new members, leaders & executive sponsors
- Planning leadership development for themselves and their successors

The most common individual roles and responsibilities are described here but should be used only for consideration by any group.

Responsibilities of the Chair or Co-Chairs

Chair roles are akin to CEO or president roles and sometimes called as such. Chairs must obtain funding according to the organization's process and then manage the group's budget according to plan. The chairs are ultimately accountable for the

---

[5] ELA offers six (6) ERG Blueprints™ that are two- or three-page fillable PDFs to help learn and plan each of the operating areas.

group's health and progress. The chairs aim to ensure successful programming, membership engagement and growth, and frictionless management operations, including group reporting and communication. They must keep each other, group members, the Diversity Office, executive sponsors and the overall employee population properly informed.

Ideally, employee groups follow a leadership succession process so that an experienced chair is always in place while another, newer co-chair learns from them. In some organizations, former leaders will be called upon to mentor or offer additional support to current leaders when needed.

Responsibilities of the Vice Chair(s), Treasurer and Secretary/Administrators

These positions depend on how many people want to be involved as leaders, the group's budget or member count, and the leadership succession plan for the group. They have the typical responsibilities of the titles, such as treasurers are tasked to track and report on budgets. Secretaries or administrators typically record meeting minutes and provide project management support.

Responsibilities of the Global, Regional and Chapter Leaders

Global, regional and chapter leaders support and coordinate multiple geographic areas, often within a hierarchy of leadership responsibility. For example, there can be Hispanic/LatinX group leaders at each regional, country and international level.

Responsibilities of the Committee Leaders

Depending on the size of the overall group, committees can help manage specific events, processes (e.g., communications, new member onboarding, leadership elections) or group governance. Committees can have multiple leadership positions (chair, vice chair, secretary), which may or may not mimic the overall group's leadership structure. A committee, for example, might have a member outreach leader for a specific initiative, but the overall group leadership team is responsible for that function in the larger group. Committee leadership roles provide learning and exposure for future employee group leaders.

Responsibilities of the Event or Program Leaders

Sometimes, individuals who are not otherwise group or committee leaders can lead a specific activity or initiative. These individuals bring their unique experience, connections or passion for a specific program, such as raising money for an affiliated charity or lending unique skills to train members. The roles are temporary in support of a specific event or have an ongoing specific function such as new member onboarding. These leadership roles can also be excellent ways to develop and showcase individuals with future group leadership potential.

Do Leaders Get Paid?

Employee group leader compensation is challenging and controversial with legal, accounting, tax and social ramifications. Paying leaders is still a hot topic in ELA forums, with both sides of the debate offering legitimate pros and cons. LinkedIn is one of the organizations that led the leader pay movement. It announced in 2021 that it would compensate its global leaders at $10,000 per annum tied to accomplishing a clear set of job responsibilities. The group leader's compensation is in addition to the leaders' regular salaries and is explicitly not to be used to replace any of their 'hired job' raises or bonuses. A handful of other organizations give smaller amounts (typically $1,500 or less) as bonuses or contingent compensation only earned while still satisfactorily performing the leadership role.

Depending on the person and the timing, additional pay may or may not change an individual leader's motivation. Yet, most organizations agree that while this work is voluntary (and therefore unpaid), it is no less deserving of recognition and tangible rewards.

In addition to or instead of cash compensation, many oversight managers are building recognition programs with one or more ways to reward leaders, such as gift cards or accrued points that can be redeemed in online marketplaces. Recognition can also include acknowledgment on social channels, internal newsletters or emails and ticker tape-type boards physically posted within the organization's facilities. ELA offers free Appreciation Shout Outs that publicly showcase contributions about any type of employee group champion, including leaders, members, executive sponsors, allies and DEI professionals. In addition to internal award events and programs, a few 3rd party organizations offer such recognition, usually requiring a fee to submit or attend. (Author's note: ELA does not do this as such programs can demotivate the groups/leaders that *do not 'win' or are less represented but no less deserving. We do not want ERG work to be unnecessarily competitive or a reflection of the loudest or best PR presented.)*

Most ELA's member organizations now hold virtual, hybrid or in-person employee group leader summits focused on professional and leadership development to recognize and mobilize leaders. Agendas include motivational speakers, outside experts and executive interaction. These meetings aim to educate and inspire the leaders, as well as reinforce that their work is valued. *See page 93, Appendix B: Sample Agenda for an Employee Group Leadership Summit.*

Leader burnout is a major concern since the role requires more than work/life balance but also conscientious work/work management. The additional responsibilities can be burdensome if not self-regulated or well-supported by the organization. Additionally, the passion that draws the employees to participate in a group leader role can drown them in ERG work, making them less effective with their hired job responsibilities. Time and project management skills are critical for successful employee group leadership. Executive sponsors, past leaders and oversight managers can be important thought partners to help prioritize leader tasks. More formal coaching or mentoring support can also be helpful.

With every keynote I do for employee group leadership events, the organizer inevitably asks me to convey the organization's sincere appreciation for these leaders' critical work. Ironically, these organizers typically ask me to remind the leaders that their roles are voluntary and to permit them to vacate the position if they are no longer willing or able to perform their duties effectively.

And, even with good application vetting, some leaders will be ineffective. They may be unprepared, not receive the support or training they need, or their personal circumstances change, making it too hard to take on the extra responsibility.

A tired or toxic group leader is worse than no leader at all. No organization can afford the negative impact of a burned-out or disgruntled leader on the other leaders, the group, or the leader's hired job responsibilities. A leader offboarding policy should be clearly defined in the organization's employee group governance for these legitimate and important reasons. All of this should be considered in the leader compensation policy, too.

Oversight managers are typically salaried employees and do not receive extra compensation for managing employee groups. However, they can and should be included in recognition and appreciation programs.

Executive sponsors are typically salaried, senior employees. They should never be financially compensated to do the employee group work but should be recognized for work well done and for their help.

Internal allies and group members should never be paid for participating in or supporting an employee group. Still, they should also be included in a recognition and rewards program to thank them for their voluntary contributions.

Members typically do not pay to participate in employee groups or group activities. However, a few rare organizations (e.g., municipalities or state agencies) have regulatory requirements that prevent organizational funding and instead, charge employees a group membership fee. These fees, like union dues, may be automatically deducted from the employees' paychecks.

How Do You Measure Employee Group Success?

Employee group data is central to documenting progress and showing success to the group itself and the broader organization. These metrics can guide funding decisions and help set priorities.

Some helpful metrics include:
- Number of employees on the group mailing list and the change in this number over time
- Number of group member chats or messages
- Average number of months members remain in the group or are active in the group
- Number of group events
- The average number of members per event
- Number of employees participating in one or multiple group activities/programs
- Money raised or donated by the group to a charitable cause or non-profit organization
- Promotions, raises or other career achievements by group members
- Number of new employees hired within a target demographic, ideally mapped to employee group participation in the hiring process
- Number of employees retained within the target demographic (whether they are members of the group or not)
- Employee engagement compared between those who are and who are not members of an employee group

The last four metrics in the above list heavily depend on a partnership between DEI and the employee group leaders to coordinate with data managed by the HR department. Cross-department collaboration can be challenging in some

organizations, limiting the type of data that can be tracked. But there are other reasons why reporting might be limited:
- There needs to be systems or processes in place to track group activities.
- Too many systems have various information, but no one can or has time to collect and combine it.
- Employee group leaders require training or are too busy to use the available systems or perform manual processes.
- No one is asking for or seems to want the data.
- Organizational or legal restrictions exist to sharing employee data such as demographic, performance and salary information.

While data is the ultimate indicator of progress and impact, employee groups should also collect anecdotal or qualitative information. A group should track any internal successes, such as a member who receives an academic scholarship because of a mentor they found within the group or a member who cites the employee group as a factor in their decision to join or stay with the organization. Outstanding groups have processes for collecting such successes, like designating a specific person to document member achievements. These stories can be as effective in showcasing group success as the numerical data since the stories show an emotional connection and indisputable proof of the group's impact.[6]

---

[6] For more insight about qualitative and quantitate employee group measurement, see *The ERG Blueprint: Collecting and Reporting Critical Metrics*. ERG Blueprints are included in all ELA membership levels.

Section 2:
Why Employee Groups Matter

What Is the Purpose of Employee Groups?

From the Employee's Perspective

Purpose & Belonging

Employee groups provide a way to connect with employees with the same demographic characteristics, lived experiences or interests. The groups allow individuals to feel camaraderie through their shared identities and experiences. Employee groups provide brave and safe spaces for members to process issues and validate their feelings and needs. Members receive and benefit equally from giving support to one another. Feeding everyone's hardwired, neurologically proven need to belong,[7] employee groups give everyone involved a sense of purpose and confidence.

Professional & Leadership Development

Employee groups can offer invaluable learning via events, training and mentoring. Whether through formal or informal programming, employee groups organize and offer optional enrichment, typically at no cost to the employees and without any requirement to report individual results to the employer. That is, employee group members can take advantage of the programs offered but are under no obligation to do so. There is no passing grade or other validation required. As such, it is in the employee groups' best interest to be highly attuned to members' needs and expectations. This awareness helps ensure the programs are well attended and measurably impactful overall.

---

[7] Dver, Alyssa. *Confidence Is a Choice*. Mind Full Press, a subsidiary of Z. Holden Bros. Publishing Group, 2020.

Career Connections & Mobility

Employee groups create opportunities for members to meet others in the organization—from various departments, locations and levels—with whom they would otherwise not have the opportunity to connect. The groups can also provide members exclusive access to senior managers and career opportunities within the organization. Employee group members can therefore leverage various helpful career role models, resources and referrals.

Voice & Involvement

Participating in business decisions is a significant reason employee groups can benefit both employee and employer, and therefore, active involvement should be encouraged, measured and celebrated by both.

From their diverse perspectives, employee groups can provide market or product ideas. More and more product managers are leaning into employee groups to provide a relatively easy and low-cost source of market insight. Employee benefits managers are also seeking input from group members to help inform which medical, financial, and overall benefit services the employer should consider to improve utilization and reduce costs for both employee and employer. These are only two of the many ways employee groups can help organizations make more inclusive, productive and profitable decisions.

From the Employer's Perspective

Support DEI Goals

Employee groups are key drivers of the organization's talent strategy when aligned well with DEI priorities (often called *pillars*). However, DEI alignment may not be as compelling to executives who value shorter-term, revenue-driving goals. The following offers data-based evidence of how well-run employee groups contribute to better bottom-line results.

Talent Acquisition

Whether it's an employer or employee-advantageous market, attracting great talent is always competitive and expensive. Therefore, organizations want to reduce recruiting friction and internal obstacles that can turn candidates off. The absence of strong employee groups can be a deal breaker.

Monster.com[8] found that 86% of job seekers say they factor an employer's DEI reputation in their job search. Across generations and other demographics, 62% of job applicants say they would reject an offer from a company that did not support DEI.

For this reason and others, employee groups must be showcased beyond just the organization's website, annual reports and press releases. Involving group members as representatives at recruiting fairs or including them in candidate interviews and other talent acquisition processes is a good start.

Employee Retention

The cost of recruiting and onboarding a new employee can be as high as $28,000,[8] a significant loss of money and time whenever an employee leaves. Employee groups can be instrumental in retaining employees and increasing their engagement and productivity contributions. Group members are often part of the organization's onboarding process to give new employees "work friend" relationships that improve retention. According to a SHRM survey, 76% of U.S. workers who have close friends at work say it makes them more likely to remain with their employer.[9]

Leadership Pipeline & Development

Employee groups feed the organization's leadership pipeline by recognizing high-potential talent and cultivating both soft- and hard-skills leadership training. They can utilize and amplify all the Learning & Development resources, as well as provide mentoring and career pathing support.

Executive sponsors also gain awareness and experience by collaborating with diverse, cross-functional employee populations to become more effective and confident as senior managers.

Market Identification & Support

Some organizations credit employee groups for identifying and perfecting lucrative niche products and services. As noted, product managers can gain low-cost, high-value insights from

---

[8] Pugh, Marie-Reine. "From Recruitment to Onboarding, What's the True Cost of Hiring Employees?" *BambooHR*, 22 June 2023, www.bamboohr.com/blog/cost-of-onboarding-calculator.

[9] Navarra, Katie. "Workplace Romances Can Be Tricky, but Friendships Boost Retention." *SHRM*, 8 Feb. 2023, www.shrm.org/resourcesandtools/hr-topics/employee-relations/pages/workplace-romances-can-be-tricky-but-friendships-boost-retention.aspx.

employee groups representing existing or target consumer markets. By leaning into employee groups for advice, connections and direct involvement, companies can diversify their partnerships and supply chains, which creates internal pride and directly benefits their customers and communities.

Higher Productivity

Emerging academic research and organizational engagement surveys from multiple ELA members show that well-run employee groups increase *overall* employee productivity and retention – for all employees, especially group members. Because employee groups have a positive impact on employee morale, they can help lower the costs associated with healthcare, absenteeism and turnover. However, the same studies indicate that poorly run groups that are not clearly and consistently supported by senior managers will drag down overall engagement and productivity. Why? When the commitment to DEI is "all talk" but not put into practice, employees feel betrayed, unvalued and their trust in management erodes.

The net-net: when organizations support employee groups in a way that the groups are strong and sustainable, the entire organization gains tangible, profitable benefits. When there are no employee groups, or they aren't supported well, it can be a significant competitive disadvantage, creating a negative culture that diminishes every employee's contribution.[10]

---

[10] "How Diversity Recruitment Will Improve Your Employer Branding." *Monster.Com*, 22 Nov. 2022, hiring.monster.com/resources/recruiting-strategies/employer-branding/diversity-recruitment-and-your-employer-brand/.

How Are Employee Groups Visible?

As a reaction to George Floyd's murder and other reported hate crimes, many organizations rushed to "color wash" their organizational structures with newly appointed Chief Diversity Officers and programs. However, many did not sufficiently fund or support these initiatives to the degree needed for measurable and lasting DEI impact. These performative reactions did not "move the needle" and instead continued to expose the organization's lack of true commitment to DEI. Therefore, employee groups serve as authentic evidence that an organization takes DEI seriously enough to invest beyond adding token representation on their "About Us" page and various public-facing channels and reports.

Employee group members are encouraged to be vocal and participate in visible processes such as new hire interviews and onboarding. Intimate, authentic ("unslick") member videos appear in job postings and corporate websites and are projected onto screens in office waiting areas. Formal corporate social responsibility (CSR) and environmental, social and governance (ESG) reports now include detailed information about employee groups. Internal, C-level reports and meetings often include employee group updates to ensure awareness at the very top. A few organizations even have their CEOs regularly meet with employee group leaders to reinforce to them and everyone else that the work is valued and appreciated.

Data-Backed Research Is Also Surfacing

Given that doctorate and post-doctorate work can take years to be vetted and published, many studies supporting the value of employee groups will finally be publicly available. Early research focused on disparities in productivity impacts between companies with healthy employee groups and companies with struggling ones. Some research explores the organizational culture impact of having or not having employee groups. At the same time, other studies examine specific types of groups and their impact on the target populations' career success. Expect to see more research from academic and business groups that will provide further, data-backed justification for why and how to implement healthy, lasting employee groups.

The Media Loves Employee Groups, Too

On any given day, Google Alerts finds twenty or more new articles posted on the internet about employee groups. Media outlets ranging from *Bloomberg News* to *Crains NY* and *The Wall Street Journal* are showcasing why and how employee groups are contributing to employee engagement and bottom-line results.[11,12,13]

Beyond corporate-issued press releases, the media are diving into case studies and discussing issues ranging from paying employee group leaders to leveraging employee groups in attracting and retaining diverse talent populations.[11,12,13]

---

[11] Eisenpress, Cara. "Employee Resource Groups Take Center Stage for DEI Engagement." *Crain's New York Business*, 19 May 2022, https://www.crainsnewyork.com/diversity-inclusion/employee-resource-groups-drive-dei-engagement-nyc-firms.

[12] Erb, Marcus. "Leaders Are Missing the Promise and Problems of Employee Resource Groups." *Great Place To Work®*, https://www.greatplacetowork.com/resources/blog/new-research-shows-leaders-are-missing-the-promise-and-problems-of-employee-resource-groups.

[13] Morris, David Paul. "Employee Resource Groups Are on the Rise at US Companies." *The Wall Street Journal*, Dow Jones & Company, 1 Nov. 2021, https://www.wsj.com/articles/why-ergs-are-on-the-rise-11635532232.

Why Are Employee Groups So Popular Now?

Although employee groups have existed since the 1960s, new factors create an urgency for building strong and sustainable groups in every organization.

The Great Resignation and Remote World of Work

Field or front-line workers, workers on factory floors or remote offices have forever faced the challenges of being distributed and disconnected. Then, everyone appreciated what it means to work remotely and alone during the Covid pandemic. In response, many employee groups rose to provide a lifeline to those colleagues struggling with isolation and absence of belonging. Today, many organizations still face resistance from employees to physically return to an office, while others decided to make remote work the operating norm. In all workplace formats, however, employee groups continue to be a source of connection and support for interested individuals.

Advocacy and Activism

With growing awareness and continuing evidence of systemic racism, coupled with the political discontent of so many individuals, employee groups give a much-needed voice to underrepresented and often suppressed employee populations. While activism implies a more hard-hitting approach to influencing social and systemic change, employee groups can provide a productive way to channel fear and anger into cooperative advocacy and action. Employee groups can bring potential workplace issues forward before they become unmanageable problems that are potentially harmful to the organization and its individuals.

Management Void

Like everyone else these past few years, managers have been overwhelmed by the impact of COVID and other chaos in the world. As political, environmental and social instability continues, many managers still need to be equipped to effectively lead and support employees with different origins and life experiences than themselves. While unconscious bias and inclusive language training can help foster more equitable ways of speaking, thinking and acting, these lessons do not ensure that all employees have the sufficient professional development and career guidance needed to improve the mindset or job opportunities within the organization.

Not a Fad or Easily Faked

Employee groups are enjoying a bit of notoriety now. However, as employee engagement continues to be challenging (e.g., quiet quitting, fear of recession and layoffs), the urgent need for well-run and well-supported employee groups will remain for the foreseeable future. This contrasts with Corporate Social Responsibility (CSR), a critical focus for organizations in the early 2000s. Since CSR needed more transparency and measurability, it led to fraudulent reporting and subsequent market mistrust.

Even though there are known challenges to accurately recording and reporting employee demographics, most organizations can measure talent acquisition and retention by at least race, age and gender—and everyone expects those to be reported general data points. Prospective employees can also read about the employer culture and employee attitudes on sites like Glassdoor.

Section 3:
Where Employee Groups Are Now and Where They're Going Next

What Is the General State of Employee Groups Today?

Employee groups have gained exponential momentum in the past few years and are now mainstream. Every organization with more than a thousand employees already has or should be actively developing employee groups. Oversight managers and offices are now the norm. ERG leader training and recognition are expected rewards of the voluntary "job." Formal success metrics are required for reporting to a variety of stakeholders; policy and governance documents must be established, systematically updated and easily accessible to all who are interested. *See page 81, Appendix A for a template to build your own Employee Group Policy & Procedures Guide.*

Also, parallel to the Corporate Social Responsibility (CSR) movement, there is a noticeable difference between organically inclusive cultures and those trying to retrofit diversity into their regular operations and culture. More specifically, the top leaders need to do more than say they respect diversity; they must lead by example and become educated about it. One way to do this is to become directly involved and support employee groups. Senior management must continuously communicate and monitor DEI as an organizational priority and be willing to share DEI progress and setbacks transparently.

What Are the Minimum Requirements to Start Employee Groups?

I often tell people to beware of ERG case studies and so-called industry best practices because what works for one organization usually does not apply to another. What worked in one organization yesterday might not even work in the same organization today. The organization's culture, size and many other variables will dictate how employee groups will run best. With that appreciation and thousands of outstanding member examples, ELA has compiled operational templates, strategies and processes that enable ERG excellence.

Drawing upon these and other third-party sources, we see some clear steps organizations can take to ensure the successful launch of an individual employee group or an entire employee group program.

DEI Pillars

"DEI pillars" are commonly used to refer to the diversity, equity and inclusion (DEI) priorities or objectives for the entire organization. The pillars provide parameters that help employee groups choose and justify programming selection and associated funding needs. The pillars can be uniquely created by the organization or adopted from one of many prescribed and popular sources, such as Dr. Robert Rodriquez's *4C Model*: culture, career, commerce and community.[14]

---

[14] Rodriguez, Robert. "Employee Resource Group Consulting and the 4C Assessment Model." DRR *Advisors*, https://www.drradvisors.com/employee-resource-group-consulting/.

Executive and Middle Management Commitment

Employee groups can only gain the required visibility and support if all levels of management are on board. Aside from the financial and physical resources needed, employees need to be granted time and focus for employee group leadership work and for members to participate. Managers might restrict time spent with employee groups to anchor the individual to their "hired job" performance or the employee can be the target of a jealous backlash from their manager or others for having gained access to executives beyond the manager's reach. Therefore, the entire management team and workforce must be educated about the groups, why they are needed, and how everyone can support the groups and employees involved with them.

New Employee Group Application Process

The Diversity Office must define the process and rules of forming an employee group. These rules should include which types of groups will be considered, the experience and commitment required for group leaders, as well as the minimum number of initial and active members needed to maintain official group status. The Diversity Office can develop this process incrementally, adding or changing rules as more is learned and decided. However, a basic set of steps should be issued and accessible early on for anyone who wants to start an employee group. The procedure should not deter someone from starting a group. Still, it should set forward the leadership and membership commitment required for obtaining financial and other organizational support. The governance process should explain how decisions will be made: who is involved, how long it should take and what happens after the application is accepted or denied.

In many cases, these rules help redirect those individuals who would be better served by forming a more casual club or affinity group. The rules also define which types of employee groups will be recognized and funded by the organization and which will be rejected despite meeting administrative requirements. Many organizations have faced complex decisions without clear policies and potential legal challenges from groups denied recognition or support. These rules should all be documented, maintained, accessible and communicated. *(See page 81, Appendix A: Template for Creating an Employee Group Policy & Procedures Guide.)*

Funding Process

As discussed in the section "What Controversial Issues Should Be Considered?" there is no standard formula for determining how much to fund an employee group. One women's group reported that they had an annual budget of $1,000 while their competitor's women's group had an annual budget over $100,000. There is also no right answer to how much funding different groups should receive, even within the *same* organization. Some organizations give all employee groups equal funding, regardless of the number of members, programs or other performance measurements. Other organizations fund groups based on their proposed programming plans or the current number of members. Some are funded in one lump sum, while others make funding decisions based on individual program requests.

Tracking group expenses is a critical role for someone on the group leadership team, too, since both overspending and underspending can create penalties for future program funding requests.

Whichever way your organization decides to provide funding, document the process and include reimbursement policies and procedures since they are likely to differ from the rules around individual employee business expenses. And no matter how or how much money is given to the groups, be clear upfront with the budget rules to reduce real liability and unnecessary frustration for everyone.

What Controversial Issues Should be Considered?

While some standard practices have emerged to help govern employee groups generally, many policy issues remain subjective. The "right" answers depend on the specific organizational culture, history, vision and intention. In other cases, an answer can be "right" for a specific organization right now but not necessarily in the future. Employee group policies and procedures should be updated based on what is happening within the organization or socio-economic situation.

Some examples of employee group policy decisions that should be revisited at least annually:
- What is the right label (ERG, BRG, other)?
- Are aggregated labels such as multicultural, Asian and caregiver ERGs, for example, inclusive or insulting?
- Should faith-based, white male, hobby, or professional skills groups be encouraged or allowed?
- Are the groups providing a good balance of both safe and brave space meeting opportunities? How can they balance the need to educate others while giving members a genuine sense of belonging?
- How can employee groups better serve people with intersectional identities?
- How can employees in different geographies be equally supported?
- What should you do for employees who choose not to participate in groups, so they do not feel alienated, excluded or penalized?

How Do You Know Whether Your Organization Is Ready to Start Employee Groups?

If your organization doesn't yet have employee groups but is considering offering them, this initial readiness checklist can be helpful:

- Employees are either requesting or receptive when presented with the idea. Verify employee sentiment with a formal survey or a few focus group meetings. Seek to understand what employees think will work best and what they hope to gain from participating in employee groups.
- At least one employee outside the HR and management teams has voiced an interest in leading a group. Confirm that the employee's commitment and capacity support the group's launch.
- Your executive management team knows what employee groups are and how they function. They should clearly understand that the groups require ongoing financial and management support. Identify who would be willing and able to serve as executive sponsors.
- You've identified someone in Human Resources (HR) who has DEI experience, is willing and able to oversee the groups, and can develop an overarching policy and procedures guide. *(See page 81, Appendix A: Template for Creating an Employee Group Policy & Procedures Guide.)*

How Do You Know if Employee Groups Will Make a Positive Difference?

Employee groups can enhance organizational culture when the groups are done well, and the culture is already healthy. Don't expect toxic managers or cutthroat performance expectations to be mitigated by newly organized employee groups. Employee groups can only enhance the culture in organizations that already demonstrate respect and appreciation for their employees. Suppose the culture is one where employees fear speaking up, learning from failure or asking basic questions. In that case, employee groups won't compensate for—and can exacerbate—those issues by creating a forum for employees to express such legitimate grievances publicly. However, if there is a genuine desire to give employees the confidence to bring their whole selves to work, employee groups are one of the best ways to liberate that human potential.

You can minimize risk and optimize the opportunity from employee groups by clearly communicating expectations upfront. The template in Appendix A can help you think through how you want these groups to run and how your organization defines success. While you might not have all the template answers to start, your organization must remain committed to iterating the guidance and measuring the groups' health quantitatively and qualitatively, so they are undoubtedly helpful for the people they serve.

Changing how people work can be easier said than done, especially for groups already in place and running well according to their own measurements. You'll likely need to give some grace and time to those groups before they conform to the organization's policies and procedures. Meanwhile, your organization should continue recognizing and funding existing groups. Set some reasonable deadlines for them to achieve official status and come into compliance. If they don't adhere to the new guidelines by then, ensure that they are aware that their group could receive lower levels of funding and support than they have now and compared to other groups that follow the guidelines. However, imposing new rules on existing groups can take a bit of time and a lot of patience. Resistance is normal and should be expected. For the sake of equity, the guidelines should be developed, adopted and monitored so that every group can be treated fairly, consistently and predictably.

Trends & Transformations in Employee Groups

As employee group standards and measures of success are being redefined rapidly, we have seen a significant transformation in the attitudes toward and best approach to running employee groups. No longer are they considered wine and cheese gatherings or casual clubs. Employee groups have shifted from "nice to have" to being a key in creating positive employee experiences. Employee groups are becoming more evolved, more mutually beneficial versions of modern labor unions.

Considering these urgent needs, we will explore some current trends from the perspective of the group leaders, the oversight managers and the organization as a whole.

Individual Employee Group Leader Trends and Transformations

Pay, Recognition and Time Boxing

The debate on whether to pay employee group leaders continues, with reasoned insights coming from both sides. Formal recognition programs and systems are commonly used to acknowledge and reward volunteer leaders for their contributions instead of cash payments. And while the concept has merit, there are potential pitfalls. Employees can "game the system" by recognizing one another. Some deserving leaders might not receive appropriate or equitable recognition. Therefore, a poorly managed rewards system can unexpectedly cost more money and have a negative cultural impact, despite the goodwill intended.

Organizations should precisely define the work and time allocated for leadership roles and overall group membership to avoid these undesirable results. Once these parameters are documented, the employee can discuss expectations with their manager and, ideally, receive a formal, written agreement. In this way, everyone is aware of the workload and commitment involved. This process includes the individual's commitment to uphold the current "hired job" performance and the manager's promise not to penalize or limit the employee's opportunities.

Many other ways are being used to recognize the work and contributions made to employee groups. Examples include annual leadership summits for special professional development, meetings with CEOs, and letters from or to senior executives that thank a group leader or team. Leaders get recognized on company portals, in DEI newsletters and through ELA Appreciation Shout Outs. We expect to see more creative and consistent ways leaders and other group contributors will be rewarded for their work instead or in addition to cash compensation.

Engagement, Coaching and Offboarding

Employee group leader engagement continues to be a major concern. In the past few years of social unrest, group leaders courageously and generously stepped up to provide safe spaces where members could talk through sensitive issues and create a place of at least virtual belonging. Yet, in the process, many leaders became burned out. Throughout 2022, HR, DEI and oversight managers continuously lamented over disengaged leaders and worried that providing formal training would overwhelm their volunteer leaders. Softer forms of support, such as coaching and wellbeing events were used to inject some motivation and compassion. But as COVID waned and hybrid work became the new norm, organizations began identifying employee group leaders who needed more structured help and rules to drive their groups forward. HR and DEI managers are now gently inviting ineffective leaders to step aside and make way for others who can lead the groups into the future.

In 2023, layoffs and reorgs added job insecurities that increased stress and removed support from these groups. Leadership roles needed to be filled. Many DEI professionals were either laid off or voluntarily left, hoping to find jobs with organizations that are truthfully committed to DEI. Meanwhile, progressive organizations are pushing ahead to have strong oversight managers running fast to offer all the above: coaching, summits, special training and networking opportunities, rewards, recognition and organizational support. They are also hustling to create intersectionality and synergy with the groups, so the sum of the leadership efforts is greater than any one of the individual groups.

ERG Leader Training

In 2023, ELA saw a significant uptick in leader training engagements. We trained thousands of leaders through workshops, keynotes, and coach-assisted learning programs. The training was often done as part of an organization's ERG Summit. Some organizations sent their leaders to ELA's Symposium, and others purchased memberships to give them self-service resources in ELA Online. In this mix of formats and knowledge levels, it was clear that all leaders must be trained quickly with measurable effectiveness. On top of all other group leadership responsibilities, the training happens on borrowed time from their hired roles. Plus, with a short tenure of 1-2 years as group leader, there is truly no time to waste.

Leaders often leave for various reasons and take critical group knowledge and experience with them. The new group leaders then waste time and energy reinventing all the processes and structures needed. Therefore, training should educate and create documentation to ensure current and future leadership alignment.

ERG Leader and Trainer Certification

As a visible data point of the importance of well-trained leaders, ELA's ERG Leader and Expert ERG Trainer Certification programs have become increasingly used by organizations to motivate and measure leadership preparedness. These official certifications provide leaders with confirmation of and confidence in their knowledge as well as an incentive to complete the requirements to gain a valuable career credential.

Organizations that sponsor leader or training certifications clearly signal their commitment to employee groups and leadership development.

Even without organizational sponsorship, ELA sees many individuals self-fund their certifications to explore consulting and future career opportunities for themselves, whether during job transitions or going from being a volunteer DEI/ERG leader to becoming a salaried DEI manager.

Employee Group Oversight Manager Trends and Transformations

Governance, Policy Guides and ESG/CSR/C-Suite Reporting

Since employee groups are funded by their organization, it is no surprise that management wants to see the groups run orderly, measurable and consistently. Documented governance outlines the rules and responsibilities within a group so everyone involved can work more efficiently by ensuring alignment and minimizing overlapping efforts. The definition of scope, charter, mission and vision, leadership structure, succession planning, budgeting and other processes are all part of a group's governance. And while the details will vary between groups and change over time for each group, solid governance provides stability and sustainability.

With the recent explosion in the popularity of the oversight manager role, it's clear that organizations see creating synergy and order across employee groups as a priority. As discussed previously, oversight managers are now typically creating policy guides or operating manuals to align expectations across groups and to inform leaders about systems, processes and resources they should use to make the work easier.

Beyond these overarching operating expectations, employee groups may also need to provide ongoing information that will be included in official corporate publications such as environmental, social and governance (ESG) and corporate social responsibility (CSR) reports. Because employee groups are highlighted in these very public documents, the groups must provide concrete metrics that demonstrate their impact on target populations as well as a quantitative return on investment. These expectations will accelerate the need for collecting and communicating group and member data. However, beyond simply substantiating their contributions toward diversity, equity and inclusion goals, we also expect to see employee groups using more and more data to help quantify their impact on the business, community, employee productivity, engagement and overall culture.

Full-time Roles, Program Offices and Local Management

In 2019, you could have counted the number of paid, professional oversight managers on one hand. Now just about any organization with more than five employee groups either has or is planning to hire someone to oversee the groups. These oversight managers can have additional diversity- or HR-related responsibilities as well.

Beyond the community learning in ELA's Oversight Manager Group (OMG), we plan and expect other formal curriculum and certification paths for these professionals that incorporate the leadership and management skills required to motivate people who are not direct reports. Job requirements include project and time management, plus more comfortable negotiating and presenting. Oversight managers also need to know how to be a coach, whether it be a group leader or executive sponsor!

Team Building, Councils and In-person Retreats

With organizations already calling for better group leader engagement and improved synergy across groups, the global COVID pandemic changed how we work and collaborate. As a result, we've seen training requests skyrocket for team-building skills that can be applied in distributed, remote, and hybrid work environments.

With the proliferation of all types of employee groups, addressing intersectionality has become a key concern for diversity leaders. Intersectionality refers to a person's overlapping identities and potential affiliations with multiple groups. A single employee, for example, might wish to participate in multiple employee groups to align with their gender, culture, and sexual orientation. But this would require them to make multiple commitments or choose among competing priorities. Therefore, organizations are challenged with managing their groups synergistically and even to co-create, attend, and promote one another's programming. While DEI councils have gained good momentum, they don't typically get involved with employee group programming and governance. Therefore, employee group councils are sprouting up to share plans, knowledge and programming costs between group leaders.

Many companies host employee group leader summits or retreats to foster greater camaraderie and recognize the importance of the work. Group leaders (sometimes also executive sponsors) convene for leadership training and group planning, online or in person. Positioned as a special professional development perk, these events often feature outside expert speakers, hands-on workshops and opportunities for executive interaction. We are thrilled to see organizations investing time and money to bolster employee groups and are excited to support the events in several ways. It can be challenging to pull group leaders away from their hired jobs to attend these events – especially on top of their expected volunteer group leadership responsibilities. Therefore, the summit events must deliver maximum value for all involved *(See page 93, Appendix B: Sample Agenda for an Employee Group Leadership Summit.)*

Organizational Trends and Transformations

International, Non-U.S. and Sub-Employee Group Categories

Larger, global organizations have led the way by having employee group structures that support their geographic footprints. As discussed previously, local, regional and global levels typically reflect a company's sales priorities more than its DEI objectives. Because the push to have employee groups around the globe has largely been driven by international companies headquartered in the U.S., the structure and operations of those groups only sometimes meet the needs of the populations they purport to serve. Often, local leaders are expected to adopt and adapt within a U.S.-centric model.

At ELA, we are excited about the number of non-U.S. organizations attending our events and requesting training. These organizations may or may not have any U.S. presence, and the pioneering individuals are wonderfully open and eager to learn and adapt lessons from employee group leaders based elsewhere. Their groups are unlikely to follow U.S. policies strictly and should instead reflect the culture and needs of the employee populations in their geographies. For example, it will be more appropriate and effective in some regions to have more precisely defined groups for Indian, Korean, Japanese, Chinese, and other national or even city-specific employee groups rather than a monolithic Asian group. While subgroups can roll up to a greater region or employee group category, each should ideally have its own governance, programming calendar and budget.

This type of sub-segmentation has also proven useful within employee groups organized around common interests. For example, a general-purpose caregivers' group cannot equally meet the needs of different subgroups: caregivers of young children, parents of adult children with disabilities, employees caring for aging parents or employees serving as foster parents. We expect to see more organizations creating narrower groups that better support the needs of their specific members.

We also expect to see programming having more respect for time zones and language (e.g., translation), accessibility (e.g., captioning and transcription), as well as more input from group leaders and members based around the world. To be truly inclusive, leaders should never assume they know what their members want, even if they have been a group member. Whether planning programming or swag, there can be vast differences in what is appropriate in one geography versus another. Even within a single geography, there are likely members with differing cultural norms, learning styles and work schedules who should also be considered in the group's plans.

Metrics, Systems, Group & Member Marketing

As noted previously, we are unsurprisingly seeing an urgency to collect data that measures employee groups' return on investment and overall progress. To enable this, software tools are flooding the market, each with their functionality and focus: organizing and tracking events, enabling member communication and budgeting. As with other enterprise software categories, such as Customer Relationship Management (CRM) and Enterprise Resource Planning (ERP), we expect the number of software offerings to consolidate, with a few key players remaining over time.

Consultants and consulting firms offer expertise to help strategically plan and execute employee group activities. Leveraging varying DEI and ERG experience levels, these service providers offer often-needed heads and hands. Buyers need to beware that the ERG space is changing so rapidly that prior experience is often quickly outdated. As noted earlier, what works for one group might not work for another, even inside the same organization. However, a consultant can still offer insight and partnership, provided they are open to change and diversity!

Marketing agencies are also in the mix, offering their expertise to promote an employee group's and its members' success. While the intention to elevate the perception of employee groups is noble, just be careful not to add too much sizzle. You'll risk losing the very heart of what employees value: trust, equality and authenticity.

DEI, Talent Acquisition and Employee Experience

Diversity professionals continue to lead the charge in moving the heavy inclusion needle, but they need to do the work with others. Talent acquisition professionals realize their success depends on demonstrating proof of the organization's commitment to DEI with hard evidence that their employee groups are real and active. Candidates want to talk directly to ERG leaders and members. They will ask about programs offered and funding allotted. They want to confirm that they aren't being hired to fill a quota but as qualified, valued contributors.

Still relatively new in many organizations, employee experience teams can also help support ERGs. These professionals aim to improve the employment lifecycle or "employee journey," from interviewing to onboarding, through career pathing, talent optimization, and even helping to educate and prepare employees for retirement or lead them through a graceful offboarding. Employee experience professionals know that healthy ERGs can increase employee engagement scores and enable more positive social posts. Strong employee groups make acquiring and retaining happy, productive talent easier.

What's Coming Next?

In every type and size of an organization, employee groups around the world are quickly forming and formalizing. The pace of change is exhilarating as new groups are created, with outstanding practices freely shared within and across organizations. With this urgency to organize, establishing operational excellence becomes critical.

Following the history of similar markets, ELA predicts that the still-nascent "ERG market" will likely consolidate and show some maturity within the next three years. In the meantime, we anticipate much noise in the marketplace, with a plethora of service and software vendors offering solutions to help develop and manage employee groups. Many of these suppliers will have direct experience leading employee groups, but that knowledge will become quickly outdated, given the pace of change we're seeing. The scalability and portability of these solutions will also be challenging, as no one case study will directly apply to another group's capabilities and needs. Each will reflect the unique culture, leadership, experience, business and diversity objectives of the organization, along with the intersecting economic, political and social pressures at that moment in time.

Expect to see variation and experimentation in all aspects of employee groups, especially with:
- Ways to recognize and reward leaders
- Measurement and promotion of group success
- Definition of all associated leadership roles and responsibilities

What Can You Do Right Now?

I hope you now clearly understand how interesting, exciting, empowering and meaningful employee groups are... and that you are inspired to join the community!

If your organization does not yet have employee groups, ask yourself and others why. Find out if there are reasons that can be overcome or if this is a clear sign that should direct your own career planning. Perhaps you are willing and able to raise your hand to start employee groups. If so, you're in great company with over 41 million other group members forging ahead with this challenging but truly rewarding work.

Please know that the ELA team is always delighted to help. We invite you to sign up on our mailing list to stay informed about the many free upcoming events and resources. If not already, consider becoming an official individual or organization member to leverage all the ERG-specific information, tools and connections. Whatever your level of involvement, we are grateful for your participation.

We work together so that everyone can belong.

Appendix A: Template for Creating an Employee Group Policy & Procedures Guide

Use this template to create your organization's own employee group guide to set policies and procedures for all your organization's groups. A completed guide should provide the rules and overall expectations for effectively running employee groups and interacting with various stakeholders, including leaders of other groups and the Diversity Office.

Feel free to use this template in whole or in part, adapting as information evolves. You may need different versions of the guide for distinct types of groups and geographies.

Please be aware that any tool will be limited in its effectiveness if not supported by a proper communication and training strategy. Neither this template nor a finished guide can eliminate the need for operational and leadership training that teaches leaders how to create their specific group governance and plans.

ELA offers training, events, workshops, keynotes and coaching for employee group leaders, oversight managers, executive sponsors and allies.

Your finished guide should be a living document easily accessible and communicated to every employee group leader and executive sponsor. You can even request that your leaders and sponsors confirm that they have received and read the guide, just as you would with an HR policy handbook. Be sure also to communicate changes or additions over time. We will continue to update this template as we compile more innovative ideas and outstanding practices from ELA members. The latest version of the template, in an editable format, is included as part of all ELA membership levels.

Please let us know if you think anything needs to be added, needs further explanation, or if you want help to create your guide.

Contact us at:

info@ERGLeadershipAlliance.com

Message From the CEO/CHRO/DEI Lead
- Purpose of the guide
- Our existing groups are and where online to find them

Our Organization's Overall ERGs' Mission and Purpose

(replace "ERG" with whatever term you use for employee groups)

- Why our organization has employee groups (employee group-specific mission/purpose/vision will be in each group's charter)
- What types of employee organizations exist in our organization, and how the employee groups are different
- Our organization's DEI pillars (e.g., 4Cs): why we have pillars, what ours specifically are and how to apply/use them in your employee group
- What we want our employee groups to do and be known for
- What we do NOT want our employee groups to do and be known for
- Who/what types of employee groups our organization supports
- What other types of employee groups our organization supports (e.g., affinity groups, clubs)
- The benefits of being an employee group leader
- The benefits of being an employee group committee leader/participant
- Why and how your employees benefit from employee group membership
- The benefits of being an executive sponsor
- Why and how allies benefit from our employee groups

- Why and how external partners (new and existing) benefit from our employee groups
- Why and how customers benefit from our employee groups
- Why and how investors benefit from our employee groups

Our Employee Group Application & Acceptance Process

- Who can apply to start an employee group?
- Does the person or people who apply then need to lead the employee group, too?
- How does someone apply to start a new employee group?
- What type of information is required to fill in the application?
- Who reviews the application? And how long does it typically take to decide?
- What happens if the employee group application is rejected?
- What happens next/needs to be done if the application is accepted?

Your Employee Group Mission and Goals

- Creating or maintaining your employee group charter to note why your employee group exists and whom you serve
- Determining your employee group's principle guiding DEI objectives or pillars for all employee groups.
- The ways we want to measure employee group progress and success

Your Employee Group Structure

- Chapters (local, national, global, etc.). Be sure to include naming conventions for each level and the corresponding leadership roles.
- Roles, responsibilities and time commitment expectations for all roles:
    - Employee group leaders/chairs
    - DEI Office
    - DEI council
    - ERG council
    - Executive sponsors
    - Members
    - Committee leads/chairs
    - "Hired job" managers
    - Allies
    - Others not associated with the employee group
- Leadership terms
- Voting/application process to elect new leaders
- Succession process and planning
- Implications (funding, etc.) if there are leadership roles not filled
- What happens when no one wants to lead?
- What happens if a leader isn't fulfilling the responsibilities?

Your Employee Group Governance Requirements

- When and how is employee group planning done?
- Who can join/be a member of an employee group?
- What is the minimum membership level required to maintain good standing?
- Are there any hired job or experience requirements to lead an employee group?

- When and how should you have employee group leadership meetings?
- Cross-employee group council meetings
- Working with oversight manager(s)
- Length of terms for leaders
- How to fill open leadership slots
- What metrics should be collected and how to report them to the oversight manager, Diversity Office, DEI council, employee group council, your executive sponsor(s), other executive committees or groups
- Confidentiality and privacy policies for the organization and employee group
- Conflict resolution between leaders and between others in the structure
- How to manage misconduct of a member
- Dissolution process

Launching Your Employee Group

- How others have launched or a suggested process to announce a new employee group
- Internal communication channels to consider using when you launch
- Required elements before you launch, such as the number of committed members, funding, first event, etc.
- How to measure a successful launch
- What happens right after the launch

The Employee Group Budget and Funding Process

- Our employee group budgeting process & systems. What information is needed to request funding, and when? If there is a form or template, please link to it.
- Our budget approval process. When and how are employee groups informed about funding decisions?
- How and when are employee group monies or reimbursements paid?
- Rules regarding employee group spending. What can employee groups buy and do (and not do) with their allocated budget?
- Method for tracking spending
- What reporting is required during a fiscal year?
- What reporting is required to use for next year's request?
- How to request funding during a fiscal year for something unexpected/originally unplanned

Communicating with Your Members

- Things you should communicate about (e.g., events, changes in leadership, surveying your members' interests)
- Our organization's writing style and any specific communication "dos" and "don'ts"
- Approval process for sending mass communications to members
- Systems/channels you can use to communicate to ERG members and others in the organization (e.g., email, Slack), including links and login information
- Systems and processes we use to plan, register members and run employee group events, including links and login information
- Systems and processes we use to do employee group reporting (e.g., event attendance, mailing list size), including links and login information
- Systems and processes for archiving member communications, including links and login information
- Process for reporting member communications (e.g., open rates, click-through rates)

Communicating with Other Employee Group Supporters

- When and how to communicate with your executive sponsor
- When and how to communicate with your oversight manager(s)
- When and how to communicate with your allies

- When and how to communicate with prospective members

How to Recruit Employee Group Members

- What are reasonable membership goals and ways to measure them?
- What are the methods and messages you can use to recruit new members?
- How to manage potential negative responses and pushback
- How can prospective members express their interest and join?
- Who should help recruit new members?
- What is the recommended member onboarding process?

How to Recruit ERG Allies

- Why allies are important to your employee group
- What are reasonable allyship goals and ways to measure them?
- What are the ways you can recruit new allies?
- Who should help recruit new allies?
- What is the recommended ally onboarding process?

How to Plan & Run Employee Group Leadership Meetings

- Frequency, purpose and length of meetings
- Who sends the agenda and how
- How to record, share and archive minutes
- How many meetings must leaders and others attend to maintain good standing?
- What is expected from the employee group leadership team, including meeting attendance requirements
- What happens if a leader misses more than is allowed?

How to Plan & Run Employee Group Programming

- When and how do you plan programming/activities for your employee group?
- What information and process are required to get programs approved?
- What metrics should be captured for every program?
- What and how should program results be reported?
- Policies for using the organization's own facilities, accounts and staff to support in-person and virtual programming activities
- Vendor hiring policies and processes, including payment, quality assurance, security, etc.

Leadership Tips

- How to balance your hired job responsibilities with your ERG work
- How to ensure that your hired job manager supports your ERG work
- Ways to motivate other leaders to get their work done

Appendix B: Sample Agenda for an Employee Group Leadership Summit

This day and a half example agenda can be used to plan a summit/retreat/ERG event to energize, educate and empower leaders of individual employee groups and their executive sponsors. The agenda aims to provide necessary operational knowledge, sustained motivation, valuable recognition and purposeful belonging. Use the agenda template to map out your own event or contact ELA to help plan and deliver it for you!

—Day 1—			
Group Leaders & Executive Sponsors			
Welcome – Introductions, Agenda & Training Objectives			10 mins
Icebreaker (See page 96 for directions to an example icebreaker: Just Like Us Scavenger Hunt)			30 mins
Keynote: "ERG Leaders are Superheroes- Brain Science Proves It"			1 hour
Break			15 mins
ERG Leaders		Executive Sponsors	
ERG Blueprint Workshop: Defining Your Group's Purpose, Leadership Process & Roles		Workshop: "How to be an Excellent Executive Sponsor"	1 hour
Break			5 mins
ERG Leaders		Executive Sponsors	
ERG Blueprint Workshop: Recruiting & Onboarding Members, Leaders & Executive Sponsors		Workshop: How to Coach Confidence	1 hour
Lunch: ERG Leaders + Executive Sponsors (Sponsors leave after lunch)			1 hour
Workshop: How to Coach Confidence			1 hour
ERG Blueprint Workshop: Selecting Programming that Best Supports Your Members, Diversity & Business Objectives			1 hour
Break			15 mins
Discussion: Enabling ERG Intersectionality — Building a joint programming calendar and other ways to support each other's groups			1 hour

—Day 2—	
Group Leaders Only	
Day 1 Debrief: questions, comments, major takeaways	15 minutes
ERG Blueprint Workshop: Informing & Engaging All of Your Group's Stakeholders	1 hour
ERG Blueprint Workshop: Collecting and Reporting Critical Group Metrics	1 hour
Break	15 minutes
ERG Blueprint Workshop: Ensuring Your Own & The Leadership Team's Development	1 hour
Group leaders work together to finish their ERG Blueprints *(Can be submitted for ERG Leader Certification)*	1 hour
Lunch	1 hour

Just Like Us Scavenger Hunt

Directions: Create a group with 3-4 other people that don't know one another. Discuss and identify a common answer to the following questions (15 mins):

- A city you all have visited
- A song you all love
- A food you all eat at least once every week
- A movie you have all watched
- The most unusual thing one of you collects
- The person who has the next birthday
- Someplace you'd all like to go someday
- Who is your group spokesperson?

Have each group spokesperson verbally their share group's answers at the end with the other participants. (1-2 minutes each group; total debrief time with transitions, 15 mins)

Acknowledgments

I fantasized a long time ago about what it would be like to only work with happy, respectful people who want to make a positive difference in the world. My dream has come true now that I get to collaborate with incredible humans all over the world who are committed to making workplace diversity, equity and inclusion a reality. DEI and ERG champions are the salt of the earth. They are compassionate, open-minded, thoughtful and generous humans who take the hard road in human resources and diversity departments. I started ELA to support them and selfishly because I really liked working with them. They give more than they take and are willing to work passionately, making personal sacrifices by taking professional risks—all so they can empower other people who have been systemically denied information, advancement and voice.

I also have the privilege of working with the ERG Leadership Alliance team, who are expertly talented yet willingly agile individuals. They respond with light speed to the challenges and opportunities of this new, evolving market. They are unquestionably responsible for their respective areas and graciously listen to my disruptive ideas that often underestimate implementation details and process interdependencies. I thank each ELA team member profusely since I know the business and this book would only exist with their contributions.

Sincerely, I want to extend the following thanks:
- To Maureen Cidzik for always making me smarter and cooler
- To Christy Andrews, who is the "can-do" glue that keeps control of what otherwise would be chaos
- To Kristy McHugh for teaching me what community and camaraderie really mean and how to do it right
- To Amy Waninger, for your patience and flexibility in working with all my book production baggage
- To Mallory Rinker for her social media stewardship
- To Bill Clement, who is the accounting umbrella to my relentless rainmaking
- To ELA's incredible cohort of Expert ERG Trainers whose own brilliance illuminates the entire team

I know scientifically that the secret to success is confident belonging. Therefore, I am only enabled by my family and their unconditional support in everything I do. I can never express how much I appreciate my husband, Jeff. He doesn't just let me do my own thing, but he does many things that empower everyone to be their best selves. I'm perpetually inspired by his commitments to his classroom, our grown-up but still-connected kids and the incredible quality of his many creative pursuits. Thank you for helping me create two spectacular young men and for patiently being a thought partner even when you are uninterested or too tired to help, but still do.

You are all why I continue to work as hard as possible to bring more real confidence to the world.

About ERG Leadership Alliance (ELA)

www.ERGLeadershipAlliance.com

The ERG Leadership Alliance (ELA) teaches Employee Resource Group (ERG) champions how to access the funding, know-how and organizational support needed to drive strong, sustainable employee groups. We offer ERG-specific training, certification, membership and connections needed to build excellent employee groups quickly and efficiently.

ELA's 25,000+ community members include oversight managers, group leaders, executive sponsors and allies. Together, we give greater voice, belonging and mobility to more than 41 million individuals already involved with ERGs around the world.

ELA's community includes most Fortune 1000, best-known non-profits, top academic institutions, state departments, and domestic and non-U.S. national agencies.

ELA Offerings

- **FREE Resources:**
    - Please attend one of our frequent public *ERG Learning Labs!*
    - Recognize someone or a team's contribution to your group with an *ERG Appreciation Shout Out.*
    - Find your dream job on the *DEI/ERG Job Board.*
    - Read the latest *ERG Trends Leadership Briefing.*
    - Review a sample *ERG Blueprint.*
    - Sign up on the *ELA mailing list* to stay aware of added resources and future events!
- **ELA Memberships:** With levels for group leaders, oversight managers or the entire organization, get access to expertly

curated ERG tools and information. Members also get discounts and tickets to ELA events, advanced access to research and advisory consultation and public recognition as a DEI pioneer.

- **ERG Leader Training**: Leaders simultaneously learn and complete plans for themselves and their groups using ELA's six (6) ERG Blueprints—various teaching formats offered, including self-service, custom workshops and coach-assisted learning.
- **ERG Leader Certification:** Leaders submit their six completed ERG Blueprints to validate and reward their knowledge. The process is quick and grants a valuable career credential.
- **Expert ERG Trainer Certification:** Achieve the ultimate validation as a recognized ERG professional and be qualified to teach the ELA curriculum within your organization as a consultant for your own or ELA's clients.
- **Keynotes:** Educate, energize and entertain ERG Leaders with tailored, brain science-based interactive presentations – a terrific way to kick off leadership summits!
- **Workshops:** Align executive sponsors and allies about employee groups, why they benefit the organization and how each person can best support the groups.
- **Symposia:** Be inspired at one of ELA's annual conferences to get invaluable knowledge and community.
- **Consulting:** Let ELA give you extra heads and hands to create your organization's ERG policy guide, ERG council and ERG member success stories.

Contact ELA at
info@ERGLeadershipAlliance.com

Made in the USA
Middletown, DE
12 May 2024